For Cath – NS

For Ashok Kachru Pandit, Musema She Hassan Yesuf and all ActionAid's children, remembering specially **Gultno Aliye** – JB

The compiler's royalties in this book are being donated to ActionAid, Hamlyn House, Archway, London N19 5PG

Oxford University Press, Walton Street, Oxford OX2 6DP

Oxford New York Toronto
Delhi Bombay Calcutta Madras Karachi
Petaling Jaya Singapore Hong Kong Tokyo
Nairobi Dar es Salaam Cape Town
Melbourne Auckland

and associated companies in
Berlin Ibadan

Oxford is a trade mark of Oxford University Press

Arrangement and Selection © Jill Bennett 1992

Illustrations © Nick Sharratt 1992

ISBN 0-19-276109-9

A CIP catalogue record for this book is available from the British Library

Printed in Hong Kong

Acknowledgements

Arnold Adoff, "My Mouth" from *Eats* (Lothrop Lee & Shepard Books, 1979). © Arnold Adoff 1979.
John Agard, "Snow-cone" from *I Din Do Nuttin* (Bodley Head, 1983). Reprinted by kind permission of John Agard c/o Caroline Sheldon Literary Agency.
Mary Ann Hoberman, "Meg's Egg" from *Oodles of Noodles* (Addison Wesley Publishing), © 1964 by Addison-Wesley Publishing Company, Inc.
Lucia & James Hymes, Jr., "Oodles of Noodles" from *Oodles of Noodles* © 1964, by Addison-Wesley Publishing Company, Inc. Reprinted with permission of the publisher.
Leland B. Jacobs, "Taste of Purple" from *Is Somewhere Always Far Away?*, © 1967 by Leland B. Jacobs. Reprinted by permission of Henry Holt and Company, Inc.
John Kitching, "I Like Cabbage", © 1991 John Kitching, first published in *Twinkle Twinkle Chocolate Bar* (OUP, 1991). Reprinted by permission of the author.
Judith Nicholls, "Brian's Picnic" and "Popalong hopcorn", © Judith Nicholls, first published in *Popcorn Pie* (Mary Glasgow Publications, 1988). Reprinted by permission of the author.
Grace Nichols, "Sugarcake Bubble" from *No Hickory, No Dickory, No Dock*, © John Agard and Grace Nichols 1991; "Have a Mango" from *Come On Into My Tropical Garden*, © Grace Nichols 1988. Reproduced with permission of Curtis Brown Group Ltd, London on behalf of Grace Nichols.
Jack Prelutsky, "Chocolate Milk" from *Rainy Day Saturday* (Greenwillow Books, a division of Wm Morrow & Company). © Jack Prelutsky.
Clive Riche, "The Wobbling Race", © 1991 Clive Riche, first published in *Twinkle Twinkle Chocolate Bar* (OUP, 1991). Reprinted by permission of the author.

Although every effort has been made to secure copyright permission prior to publication this has not proved possible in some instances. If notified the publisher will be pleased to rectify any errors or omissions at the earliest opportunity.

TASTY
POEMS

Collected by Jill Bennett
Illustrated by Nick Sharratt

Oxford University Press

Meg's egg

Meg
Likes
A *re*gular egg
Not a poached
Or a fried
But a *re*gular egg
Not a devilled
Or coddled
Or scrambled
Or boiled
But an *egg*ular egg
*Me*gular
*Re*gular
Egg!

Mary Ann Hoberman

Sugarcake bubble

Sugarcake, Sugarcake
    Bubbling in a pot
Bubble, Bubble Sugarcake
    Bubble thick and hot

Sugarcake, Sugarcake
    Spice and coconut
Sweet and sticky
    Brown and gooey

I could eat the lot.

Grace Nichols

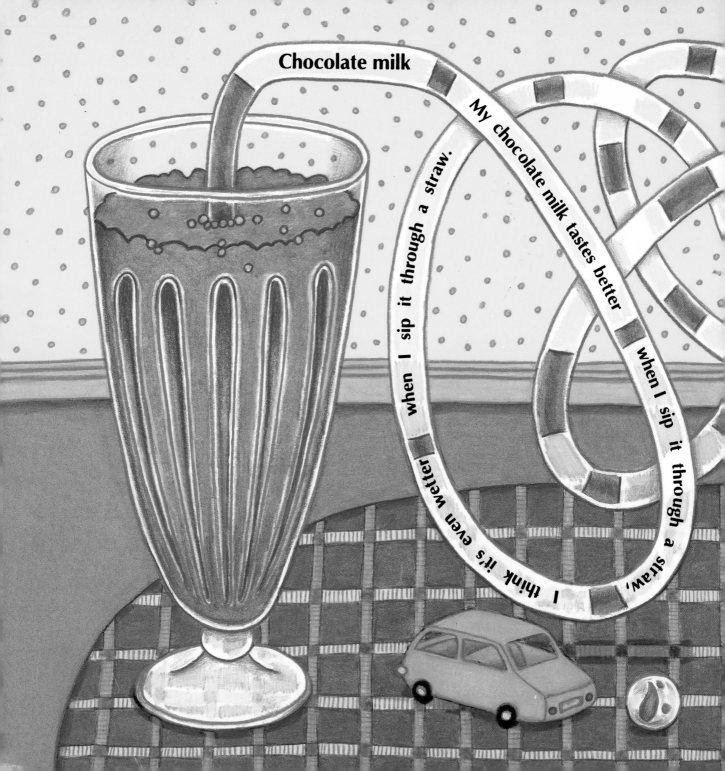

Chocolate milk

My chocolate milk tastes better when I sip it through a straw. My chocolate milk tastes better when I sip it through a straw. I think it's even wetter when I sip it through a straw.

With one end in the chocolate milk, the other at my lips, I drink up every single drop with little tickling sips.

Jack Prelutsky

Taste of purple

Grapes hang purple
In their bunches,
Ready for
September lunches.
Gather them, no
minutes wasting.
Purple is
Delicious tasting.

Leland B. Jacobs

Oodles of noodles

I love noodles. Give me oodles.
Make a mound up to the sun.
Noodles are my favourite foodles.
I eat noodles by the ton.

Lucia & James L. Hymes, Jr.

I like cabbage

I like eating cabbage,
Turnip, beetroot, cress,
Very smelly foreign cheese,
And, best, (you'll never guess)
It isn't chocolate or ice-cream,
No, no, it isn't custard,
My very best, my favourite food,
Is sausages with mustard.

John Kitching

Snow-cone

Snow-cone nice
Snow-cone sweet
Snow-cone is crush ice
and good for the heat.

When sun really hot
and I thirsty a lot,
Me alone,
Yes me alone,
could eat ten snow-cone.

If you think is lie I tell
wait till you hear the snow-cone bell,
wait till you hear the snow-cone bell.

John Agard

Brian's picnic

We've . . .
   cheese rolls, chicken rolls,
   beef rolls, ham;
   choose now, quickly, Brian —
bacon, beans or Spam?

I WANT A DOUGHNUT!

We've . . .
   egg and cress and sausages,
   good old lettuce leaf;
   come on, Brian, take some now —
   there's turkey, tuna, beef . . .

I WANT A DOUGHNUT!

We've . . .
   treacle tart and apple tart,
   biscuits, blackberries, cake —
   Take which one you feel like,
   Brian, come along now, take!

I WANT A DOUGHNUT!

There's . . .
   jelly next or trifle,
   everything must go!
   Quickly, Brian, pass your plate —
   is it yes or no?

I WANT A DOUGHNUT!

LAST CHANCE!

We've . . .
   sponge cake, fruit cake,
   eat it *any* way!
   Peanut butter, best rump steak . . .
   what is that you say?

I WANT A DOUGHNUT!

Judith Nicholls

The wobbling race

Two jellies had a wobbling race
To see who was the wibbliest.
Then the sun came out and melted them
And made them both the dribbliest.

Clive Riche

Have a mango

Have a mango
sweet rainwashed
sunripe mango
that the birds
themselves
woulda pick
if only they
had seen it —
a rosy miracle

Here

take it from mih hand.

Grace Nichols

Popalong hopcorn!

I'm a hopalong
      popalong
popcorn in the pan!

        In
   out
      up
        down!
Catch me
      if
you
         can!

Judith Nicholls

My mouth

stays shut
          but
food just
finds
          a way

                  my tongue says
we are
          full today
          but
                  teeth just
                          grin
          and
          say
                  come in

i am always hungry

Arnold Adoff

Where's Brian?